MW01097836

1		
2		
3		
4		
5		
6		
7		
8		
9		
10		
11		
12		
13		
14		
15		
16		
17		
18		
19		
20		

21		
22		
23		
24		
25		
26		
27		
28		
29		
30		
31		
32		
33		
34		
35		
36		
37		
38		
39		
40		

41		
42		
43		
44		
45		
46		
47		
48		
49		
50		
51		
52		
53		
54		
55		
56		
57		
58		
59		
60		

61		
62		
63		
64		
65		
66		
67		
68		
69		
70		
71		
72		
73		
74		
75		
76		
77		
78		
79		
80		

81		
82		
83		
84		
85		
86		
87		
88		
89		
90		
91		
92		
93		
94		
95		
96		
97		
98		
99		
100		

Book Title ______________________

Author ______________________ Nationality ______________________

Genre ______________________ Year ______________________ Pages ____________

Memorable Quote	Page Number

Characters

Plot Summary

Notes

Rating ☆ ☆ ☆ ☆ ☆

Book Title

Author

Nationality

Genre

Year

Pages

Memorable Quote	Page Number

Characters

Plot Summary

Notes

Rating ☆ ☆ ☆ ☆ ☆

Book Title

Author

Nationality

Genre

Year

Pages

Memorable Quote	Page Number

Characters

Plot Summary

Notes

Rating ☆ ☆ ☆ ☆ ☆

Book Title ______________________

Author ______________________ Nationality ______________________

Genre ______________________ Year ______________________ Pages ______________________

Memorable Quote	Page Number

Characters

Plot Summary

Notes

Rating ☆ ☆ ☆ ☆ ☆

Book Title ______________________

Author ______________________ Nationality ______________________

Genre ______________________ Year ______________________ Pages __________

Memorable Quote	Page Number

Characters

Plot Summary

Notes

Rating ☆ ☆ ☆ ☆ ☆

Book Title

6

Author

Nationality

Genre

Year

Pages

Memorable Quote	Page Number

Characters

Plot Summary

Notes

Rating ☆ ☆ ☆ ☆ ☆

Book Title ____________________

Author ________________ Nationality ____________

Genre ________________ Year ____________ Pages ______

Memorable Quote	Page Number

Characters

Plot Summary

Notes

Rating ☆ ☆ ☆ ☆ ☆

Book Title ______________________________

Author ______________________ Nationality ______________________

Genre ______________________ Year ______________________ Pages ____________

Memorable Quote	Page Number

Characters

Plot Summary

Notes

Rating ☆ ☆ ☆ ☆ ☆

Book Title ____________________

Author ____________________ Nationality ____________________

Genre ____________________ Year ____________________ Pages __________

Memorable Quote	Page Number

Characters

Plot Summary

Notes

Rating ☆ ☆ ☆ ☆ ☆

10

Book Title

Author

Nationality

Genre

Year

Pages

Memorable Quote	Page Number

Characters

Plot Summary

Notes

Rating ☆ ☆ ☆ ☆ ☆

Book Title ______________________

Author ______________________ Nationality ______________________

Genre ______________________ Year ______________________ Pages ______________________

Memorable Quote	Page Number

Characters

Plot Summary

Notes

Rating ☆ ☆ ☆ ☆ ☆

Book Title ____________________

Author ____________________ Nationality ____________________

Genre ____________________ Year ____________________ Pages __________

Memorable Quote	Page Number

Characters

Plot Summary

Notes

Rating ☆ ☆ ☆ ☆ ☆

Book Title ____________________

Author ____________________ Nationality ____________________

Genre ____________________ Year ____________________ Pages ____________________

Memorable Quote	Page Number

Characters

Plot Summary

Notes

Rating ☆ ☆ ☆ ☆ ☆

Book Title ______________________________

Author ______________________ Nationality ______________________

Genre ______________________ Year ______________________ Pages ____________

Memorable Quote	Page Number

Characters

Plot Summary

Notes

Rating ☆ ☆ ☆ ☆ ☆

Book Title ______________________

Author ______________________ Nationality ______________________

Genre ______________________ Year ______________________ Pages ____________

Memorable Quote	Page Number

Characters

Plot Summary

Notes

Rating ☆ ☆ ☆ ☆ ☆

Book Title ____________________ 16

Author ____________________ Nationality ____________________

Genre ____________________ Year ____________________ Pages ____________________

Memorable Quote	Page Number

Characters

Plot Summary

Notes

Rating ☆ ☆ ☆ ☆ ☆

Book Title ______________________

Author ______________________ Nationality ______________________

Genre ______________________ Year ______________________ Pages ____________

Memorable Quote	Page Number

Characters

Plot Summary

Notes

Rating ☆ ☆ ☆ ☆ ☆

Book Title ______________________

Author ______________________ Nationality ______________________

Genre ______________________ Year ______________________ Pages ____________

Memorable Quote	Page Number

Characters

Plot Summary

Notes

Rating ☆ ☆ ☆ ☆ ☆

19

Book Title ______________________

Author ______________________ Nationality ______________________

Genre ______________________ Year ______________________ Pages ____________

Memorable Quote	Page Number

Characters

Plot Summary

Notes

Rating ☆ ☆ ☆ ☆ ☆

Book Title ______________________

Author ______________________ Nationality ______________________

Genre ______________________ Year ______________________ Pages __________

Memorable Quote	Page Number

Characters

Plot Summary

Notes

Rating ☆ ☆ ☆ ☆ ☆

Book Title ______________________

Author ______________________ Nationality ______________________

Genre ______________________ Year ______________________ Pages __________

Memorable Quote	Page Number

Characters

Plot Summary

Notes

Rating ☆ ☆ ☆ ☆ ☆

Book Title ____________________

Author ____________________ Nationality ____________________

Genre ____________________ Year ____________________ Pages ____________

Memorable Quote	Page Number

Characters

Plot Summary

Notes

Rating ☆ ☆ ☆ ☆ ☆

Book Title ____________________

Author ____________________ Nationality ____________________

Genre ____________________ Year ____________________ Pages ____________________

Memorable Quote	Page Number

Characters

Plot Summary

Notes

Rating ☆ ☆ ☆ ☆ ☆

Book Title

Author

Nationality

Genre

Year

Pages

Memorable Quote	Page Number

Characters

Plot Summary

Notes

Rating ☆ ☆ ☆ ☆ ☆

25

Book Title ____________________

Author ____________________ Nationality ____________________

Genre ____________________ Year ____________________ Pages __________

Memorable Quote	Page Number

Characters

Plot Summary

Notes

Rating ☆ ☆ ☆ ☆ ☆

26

Book Title

Author

Nationality

Genre

Year

Pages

Memorable Quote	Page Number

Characters

Plot Summary

Notes

Rating ☆ ☆ ☆ ☆ ☆

Book Title

Author

Nationality

Genre

Year

Pages

Memorable Quote	Page Number

Characters

Plot Summary

Notes

Rating ☆ ☆ ☆ ☆ ☆

28

Book Title

Author

Nationality

Genre

Year

Pages

Memorable Quote	Page Number

Characters

Plot Summary

Notes

Rating ☆ ☆ ☆ ☆ ☆

29

Book Title ______________________

Author ______________________ Nationality ______________________

Genre ______________________ Year ______________________ Pages __________

Memorable Quote	Page Number

Characters

Plot Summary

Notes

Rating ☆ ☆ ☆ ☆ ☆

30

Book Title

Author

Nationality

Genre

Year

Pages

Memorable Quote	Page Number

Characters

Plot Summary

Notes

Rating ☆ ☆ ☆ ☆ ☆

31

Book Title ____________________

Author ____________________ Nationality ____________________

Genre ____________________ Year ____________________ Pages ____________

Memorable Quote	Page Number

Characters

Plot Summary

Notes

Rating ☆ ☆ ☆ ☆ ☆

Book Title

Author

Nationality

Genre

Year

Pages

Memorable Quote	Page Number

Characters

Plot Summary

Notes

Rating ☆ ☆ ☆ ☆ ☆

33

Book Title

Author

Nationality

Genre

Year

Pages

Memorable Quote	Page Number

Characters

Plot Summary

Notes

Rating

Book Title

34

Author

Nationality

Genre

Year

Pages

Memorable Quote	Page Number

Characters

Plot Summary

Notes

Rating ☆ ☆ ☆ ☆ ☆

35

Book Title ____________________

Author ____________________ Nationality ____________________

Genre ____________________ Year ____________________ Pages ____________________

Memorable Quote	Page Number

Characters

Plot Summary

Notes

Rating ☆ ☆ ☆ ☆ ☆

Book Title

36

Author

Nationality

Genre

Year

Pages

Memorable Quote	Page Number

Characters

Plot Summary

Notes

Rating ☆ ☆ ☆ ☆ ☆

Book Title ______________________

Author ______________________ Nationality ______________________

Genre ______________________ Year ______________________ Pages __________

Memorable Quote	Page Number

Characters

Plot Summary

Notes

Rating ☆ ☆ ☆ ☆ ☆

38

Book Title

Author

Nationality

Genre

Year

Pages

Memorable Quote	Page Number

Characters

Plot Summary

Notes

Rating ☆ ☆ ☆ ☆ ☆

39

Book Title ____________________

Author ____________________ Nationality ____________________

Genre ____________________ Year ____________________ Pages ____________________

Memorable Quote	Page Number

Characters

Plot Summary

Notes

Rating ☆ ☆ ☆ ☆ ☆

40

Book Title ______________________________

Author ____________________ Nationality ____________________

Genre ____________________ Year ____________________ Pages __________

Memorable Quote	Page Number

Characters

Plot Summary

Notes

Rating ☆ ☆ ☆ ☆ ☆

Book Title ______

Author ______ Nationality ______

Genre ______ Year ______ Pages ______

Memorable Quote	Page Number

Characters

Plot Summary

Notes

Rating ☆ ☆ ☆ ☆ ☆

Book Title ______________________

Author ______________________ Nationality ______________________

Genre ______________________ Year ______________________ Pages ____________

Memorable Quote	Page Number

Characters

Plot Summary

Notes

Rating ☆ ☆ ☆ ☆ ☆

43

Book Title ______________________

Author ______________________ Nationality ______________________

Genre ______________________ Year ______________________ Pages ____________

Memorable Quote	Page Number

Characters

Plot Summary

Notes

Rating ☆ ☆ ☆ ☆ ☆

44

Book Title ______________________

Author ______________________ Nationality ______________________

Genre ______________________ Year ______________________ Pages ____________

Memorable Quote	Page Number

Characters

Plot Summary

Notes

Rating ☆ ☆ ☆ ☆ ☆

45

Book Title

Author

Nationality

Genre

Year

Pages

Memorable Quote	Page Number

Characters

Plot Summary

Notes

Rating ☆ ☆ ☆ ☆ ☆

Book Title

Author

Nationality

Genre

Year

Pages

Memorable Quote	Page Number

Characters

Plot Summary

Notes

Rating ☆ ☆ ☆ ☆ ☆

Book Title ______________________

Author ______________________ Nationality ______________________

Genre ______________________ Year ______________________ Pages __________

Memorable Quote	Page Number

Characters

Plot Summary

Notes

Rating ☆ ☆ ☆ ☆ ☆

48

Book Title ______________________

Author ______________________ Nationality ______________________

Genre ______________________ Year ______________________ Pages ______________________

Memorable Quote	Page Number

Characters

Plot Summary

Notes

Rating ☆ ☆ ☆ ☆ ☆

49

Book Title ______________________

Author ______________________ Nationality ______________________

Genre ______________________ Year ______________________ Pages __________

Memorable Quote	Page Number

Characters

Plot Summary

Notes

Rating ☆ ☆ ☆ ☆ ☆

Book Title ______________________

50

Author ______________________ Nationality ______________________

Genre ______________________ Year ______________________ Pages __________

Memorable Quote	Page Number

Characters

Plot Summary

Notes

Rating ☆ ☆ ☆ ☆ ☆

51

Book Title ______________________

Author ______________________ Nationality ______________________

Genre ______________________ Year ______________________ Pages __________

Memorable Quote	Page Number

Characters

Plot Summary

Notes

Rating ☆ ☆ ☆ ☆ ☆

52

Book Title

Author

Nationality

Genre

Year

Pages

Memorable Quote	Page Number

Characters

Plot Summary

Notes

Rating ☆ ☆ ☆ ☆ ☆

Book Title ______________________

Author ______________________ Nationality ______________________

Genre ______________________ Year ______________________ Pages __________

Memorable Quote	Page Number

Characters

Plot Summary

Notes

Rating ☆ ☆ ☆ ☆ ☆

54

Book Title ______________________

Author ______________________ Nationality ______________________

Genre ______________________ Year ______________________ Pages ____________

Memorable Quote	Page Number

Characters

Plot Summary

Notes

Rating ☆ ☆ ☆ ☆ ☆

55

Book Title ____________________

Author ____________________ Nationality ____________________

Genre ____________________ Year ____________________ Pages __________

Memorable Quote	Page Number

Characters

Plot Summary

Notes

Rating ☆ ☆ ☆ ☆ ☆

Book Title ______________________

Author ______________________ Nationality ______________________

Genre ______________________ Year ______________________ Pages ____________

Memorable Quote	Page Number

Characters

Plot Summary

Notes

Rating ☆ ☆ ☆ ☆ ☆

Book Title ____________________

Author ____________________ Nationality ____________________

Genre ____________________ Year ____________________ Pages __________

Memorable Quote	Page Number

Characters

Plot Summary

Notes

Rating ☆ ☆ ☆ ☆ ☆

Book Title

Author

Nationality

Genre

Year

Pages

Memorable Quote	Page Number

Characters

Plot Summary

Notes

Rating ☆ ☆ ☆ ☆ ☆

Book Title ______________________

Author ______________ Nationality ______________

Genre ______________ Year ______________ Pages ________

Memorable Quote	Page Number

Characters

Plot Summary

Notes

Rating ☆ ☆ ☆ ☆ ☆

Book Title

Author

Nationality

60

Genre

Year

Pages

Memorable Quote	Page Number

Characters

Plot Summary

Notes

Rating ☆ ☆ ☆ ☆ ☆

61

Book Title

Author

Nationality

Genre

Year

Pages

Memorable Quote	Page Number

Characters

Plot Summary

Notes

Rating ☆ ☆ ☆ ☆ ☆

Book Title

Author

Nationality

Genre

Year

Pages

Memorable Quote	Page Number

Characters

Plot Summary

Notes

Rating ☆ ☆ ☆ ☆ ☆

Book Title

Author

Nationality

Genre

Year

Pages

Memorable Quote	Page Number

Characters

Plot Summary

Notes

Rating ☆ ☆ ☆ ☆ ☆

64

Book Title

Author

Nationality

Genre

Year

Pages

Memorable Quote	Page Number

Characters

Plot Summary

Notes

Rating ☆ ☆ ☆ ☆ ☆

65

Book Title ______________________

Author ______________________ Nationality ______________________

Genre ______________________ Year ______________________ Pages __________

Memorable Quote	Page Number

Characters

Plot Summary

Notes

Rating ☆ ☆ ☆ ☆ ☆

Book Title ______________________

Author ______________________ Nationality ______________________

Genre ______________________ Year ______________________ Pages ____________

Memorable Quote	Page Number

Characters

Plot Summary

Notes

Rating ☆ ☆ ☆ ☆ ☆

Book Title ______________________

Author ______________________ Nationality ______________________

Genre ______________________ Year ______________________ Pages ______________________

Memorable Quote	Page Number

Characters

Plot Summary

Notes

Rating ☆ ☆ ☆ ☆ ☆

68

Book Title ______________________________

Author ______________________ Nationality ______________

Genre ______________________ Year ______________ Pages ________

Memorable Quote	Page Number

Characters

Plot Summary

Notes

Rating ☆ ☆ ☆ ☆ ☆

Book Title ______________________

Author ______________________ Nationality ______________________

Genre ______________________ Year ______________________ Pages __________

Memorable Quote	Page Number

Characters

Plot Summary

Notes

Rating ☆ ☆ ☆ ☆ ☆

70

Book Title

Author

Nationality

Genre

Year

Pages

Memorable Quote	Page Number

Characters

Plot Summary

Notes

Rating ☆ ☆ ☆ ☆ ☆

71

Book Title ______________________

Author ______________________ Nationality ______________________

Genre ______________________ Year ______________________ Pages ____________

Memorable Quote	Page Number

Characters

Plot Summary

Notes

Rating ☆ ☆ ☆ ☆ ☆

Book Title ____________________

Author ____________________ Nationality ____________________

Genre ____________________ Year ____________________ Pages __________

Memorable Quote	Page Number

Characters

Plot Summary

Notes

Rating ☆ ☆ ☆ ☆ ☆

Book Title ____________________

Author ____________________ Nationality ____________________

Genre ____________________ Year ____________________ Pages __________

Memorable Quote	Page Number

Characters

Plot Summary

Notes

Rating ☆ ☆ ☆ ☆ ☆

74

Book Title ____________________

Author ____________________ Nationality ____________________

Genre ____________________ Year ____________________ Pages __________

Memorable Quote	Page Number

Characters

Plot Summary

Notes

Rating ☆ ☆ ☆ ☆ ☆

75

Book Title ______

Author ______ Nationality ______

Genre ______ Year ______ Pages ______

Memorable Quote	Page Number

Characters

Plot Summary

Notes

Rating ☆ ☆ ☆ ☆ ☆

Book Title

76

Author

Nationality

Genre

Year

Pages

Memorable Quote	Page Number

Characters

Plot Summary

Notes

Rating ☆ ☆ ☆ ☆ ☆

Book Title ______________________

Author ______________________ Nationality ______________________

Genre ______________________ Year ______________________ Pages ____________

Memorable Quote	Page Number

Characters

Plot Summary

Notes

Rating ☆ ☆ ☆ ☆ ☆

78

Book Title

Author

Nationality

Genre

Year

Pages

Memorable Quote	Page Number

Characters

Plot Summary

Notes

Rating ☆ ☆ ☆ ☆ ☆

79

Book Title ______________________

Author ______________________ Nationality ______________________

Genre ______________________ Year ______________________ Pages ____________

Memorable Quote	Page Number

Characters

Plot Summary

Notes

Rating ☆ ☆ ☆ ☆ ☆

80

Book Title

Author

Nationality

Genre

Year

Pages

Memorable Quote	Page Number

Characters

Plot Summary

Notes

Rating ☆ ☆ ☆ ☆ ☆

Book Title

Author

Nationality

Genre

Year

Pages

Memorable Quote	Page Number

Characters

Plot Summary

Notes

Rating ☆ ☆ ☆ ☆ ☆

Book Title

Author ______ Nationality ______

Genre ______ Year ______ Pages ______

Memorable Quote	Page Number

Characters

Plot Summary

Notes

Rating ☆ ☆ ☆ ☆ ☆

Book Title ____________________

Author ____________________ Nationality ____________________

Genre ____________________ Year ____________________ Pages ____________

Memorable Quote	Page Number

Characters

Plot Summary

Notes

Rating ☆ ☆ ☆ ☆ ☆

84

Book Title ______________________

Author ______________________ Nationality ______________________

Genre ______________________ Year ______________________ Pages __________

Memorable Quote	Page Number

Characters

Plot Summary

Notes

Rating ☆ ☆ ☆ ☆ ☆

85

Book Title

Author

Nationality

Genre

Year

Pages

Memorable Quote	Page Number

Characters

Plot Summary

Notes

Rating ☆ ☆ ☆ ☆ ☆

Book Title ______________________________

Author ______________________ Nationality ______________________

Genre ______________________ Year ______________________ Pages __________

Memorable Quote	Page Number

Characters

Plot Summary

Notes

Rating ☆ ☆ ☆ ☆ ☆

87

Book Title

Author ______________________ Nationality ______________________

Genre ______________________ Year ______________________ Pages ____________

Memorable Quote	Page Number

Characters

Plot Summary

Notes

Rating ☆ ☆ ☆ ☆ ☆

Book Title

Author

Nationality

Genre

Year

Pages

Memorable Quote	Page Number

Characters

Plot Summary

Notes

Rating ☆ ☆ ☆ ☆ ☆

Book Title ______________________

Author ______________________ Nationality ______________________

Genre ______________________ Year ______________________ Pages __________

Memorable Quote	Page Number

Characters

Plot Summary

Notes

Rating ☆ ☆ ☆ ☆ ☆

Book Title

90

Author

Nationality

Genre

Year

Pages

Memorable Quote	Page Number

Characters

Plot Summary

Notes

Rating

Book Title ______________________

Author ______________________ Nationality ______________________

Genre ______________________ Year ______________________ Pages __________

Memorable Quote	Page Number

Characters

Plot Summary

Notes

Rating ☆ ☆ ☆ ☆ ☆

Book Title

Author

Nationality

Genre

Year

Pages

Memorable Quote	Page Number

Characters

Plot Summary

Notes

Rating ☆ ☆ ☆ ☆ ☆

93

Book Title

Author

Nationality

Genre

Year

Pages

Memorable Quote	Page Number

Characters

Plot Summary

Notes

Rating ☆ ☆ ☆ ☆ ☆

94

Book Title

Author ______ Nationality ______

Genre ______ Year ______ Pages ______

Memorable Quote	Page Number

Characters

Plot Summary

Notes

Rating ☆ ☆ ☆ ☆ ☆

Book Title ______________________

Author ______________________ Nationality ______________________

Genre ______________________ Year ______________________ Pages ____________

Memorable Quote	Page Number

Characters

Plot Summary

Notes

Rating ☆ ☆ ☆ ☆ ☆

96

Book Title ______________________

Author ______________________ Nationality ______________________

Genre ______________________ Year ______________________ Pages ____________

Memorable Quote	Page Number

Characters

Plot Summary

Notes

Rating ☆ ☆ ☆ ☆ ☆

Book Title

Author

Nationality

Genre

Year

Pages

Memorable Quote	Page Number

Characters

Plot Summary

Notes

Rating ☆ ☆ ☆ ☆ ☆

Book Title ______________________

Author ______________________ Nationality ______________________

Genre ______________________ Year ______________________ Pages ____________

Memorable Quote	Page Number

Characters

Plot Summary

Notes

Rating ☆ ☆ ☆ ☆ ☆

Book Title ______________________

Author ______________________ Nationality ______________________

Genre ______________________ Year ______________________ Pages ____________

Memorable Quote	Page Number

Characters

Plot Summary

Notes

Rating ☆ ☆ ☆ ☆ ☆

Book Title ____________________

Author ____________________ Nationality ____________________

Genre ____________________ Year ____________________ Pages ____________________

Memorable Quote	Page Number

Characters

Plot Summary

Notes

Rating ☆ ☆ ☆ ☆ ☆

Made in the USA
Coppell, TX
06 September 2022

82721789R00059